Workbook Files

All workbook files can be accessed by creating an account at Excel Genius. To create an account, open your web browser and go to www.excelgenius.co/Training (notice that it is .CO not .COM). Click on Client Registration and provide your details. Once you register you will have access to the Training Workbook.xls. You can also upload your completed workbook, and upon review I will upload a certificate of completion. This page gives you an option to private message me as well, and I will respond within 24-48 hours.

*D*edicated to those who think I am a Grand Master or Sorcerer for the work I do in Excel. Also to my mother and father who have encouraged me to never stop learning.

Excel Genius - Level 1 - Ledger Path

Table of Contents

Introduction

A lot of people are terrified of starting with a blank workbook, but you have taken the first step to overcoming this fear by purchasing this book. We will begin this series with an introduction, even if you have used Excel before and think "I already know that", I encourage you to read and walk through every part of the lesson. You may learn something new or a new way of doing things.

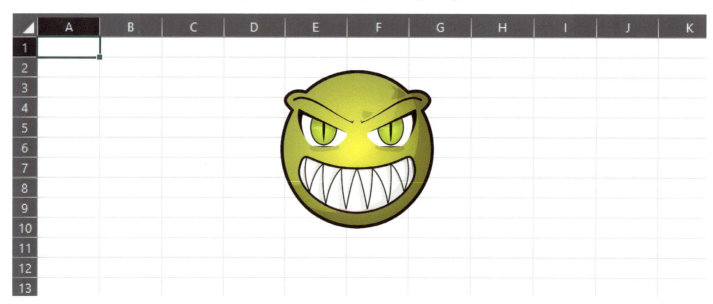

In this 4 part series, I will be walking you through the creation of an actual ledger that you can use for your personal or business finances. Once you create this it is free to use however you wish. In Lesson 1 we will create the actual ledger, after going through the features and applications of Microsoft Excel®. After this lesson you will no longer fear the blank workbook.

Excel Genius - Level 1 - Ledger Path

Getting Microsoft Excel

If you already have a version of Excel (2010 or later) you can skip this section.

There are a lot of options to get Microsoft Excel on your computer. Recently, Microsoft released Office 365, which allows you to pay monthly (1 year commitment required) . You get an online version, and depending on the plan you select you can also download the latest Full Feature desktop program as well. Most of this lesson can be done in the online lesson, however; there will be a few features not available once we get to lessons 3 and 4. I highly recommend you use the desktop version throughout the course. As a Microsoft Partner, I offer plans on my website as well. Go to www.excelgenius.co/MSO_Plans for more information.

The version you get should be based on what you can afford. It is a lot cheaper to purchase the Desktop Version however the upfront cost is quite a bit more. Once you purchase the Desktop Version you are not charged monthly, however; you are charged for upgrades and new releases.

If you cannot afford either version, most public libraries have the Microsoft Office Suite installed on their computers. You can use them to follow along in this course.

Now that you know how to get Microsoft Excel -

Let's Get It Installed!

Installing Excel

 This Section is Extremely Boring. You may need a cup of coffee to make it through.

 Computers vary by manufacturer and this guide assumes you are using Microsoft Windows 2010.

System Requirements for Office 2016[1]

COMPONENT	REQUIREMENT
Computer and processor	1 gigahertz (GHz) or faster x86-bit or x64-bit processor with SSE2 instruction set
Memory	2 GB RAM
Hard disk	3.0 GB available disk space
Display	1280 x 800 screen resolution
Graphics	Graphics hardware acceleration requires a DirectX 10 graphics card.
Operating system	Windows 10, Windows 8.1, Windows 8, Windows 7 Service Pack 1, Windows 10 Server, Windows Server 2012 R2, Windows Server 2012, or Windows Server 2008 R2 For the best experience, use the latest version of any operating system.
Browser	The current or immediately previous version of Internet Explorer; the current version of Microsoft Edge, Safari, Chrome, or Firefox
.NET version	.NET 3.5 required. Some features may require .NET 4.0, 4.5, or 4.6 CLR to also be installed.
Other	Internet functionality requires an Internet connection. Fees may apply. A touch-enabled device is required to use any multi-touch functionality. But, all features and functionality are always available by using a keyboard, mouse, or other standard or accessible input device. Note that touch features are optimized for use with Windows 8, Windows 8.1 or Windows 10. Product functionality and graphics may vary based on your system configuration. Some features may require additional or advanced hardware or server connectivity.

[1] Requirements obtained from https://products.office.com/en-us/office-system-requirements to ensure compliance with Microsoft requirements.

Installing Excel

Office for business

Not sure you can install Office? See, What product or license do I have?

Step 1. Go to portal.office.com/OLS/MySoftware.

Step 2. Sign in with your work or school account.

Step 3. On Manage installs, select **Install**.

Want to reinstall or install Office on another computer?
Go back to **Step 1**.

Office for home

Is this a new install that came with a product key? Go to office.com/setup and redeem your key.

Step 1. Go to www.office.com/myaccount.

Step 2. Sign in with your Microsoft account.

Step 3. On My Office Account, select **Install**.

Want to reinstall or install Office on another computer?
Go back to **Step 1**.

For detailed instructions to https://support.office.com and search for office installation instructions.

[1] Instructions obtained from www.office.com to ensure compliance with Microsoft Installation Instructions.

Page 7   Excel Genius - Level 1 - Ledger Path   © 2016 All Rights Reserved

Starting Microsoft Excel

So now you have a working version of Microsoft Excel on your computer. We are going to look for a shortcut to open Microsoft Excel. You should be able to find this in your start menu by clicking the Start Menu, search for Excel. Once you find it you may want to right click and pin to your taskbar or start menu.

Assuming you are using Microsoft Office 2016, once you launch the program it will take you to a start page where you have several options. Your recent spreadsheets will appear on the left and there are several templates to the right. In most cases we will open a blank workbook. I don't like the limitations of using predefined templates, but they are sometimes good for giving you ideas for your own workbooks. Let's go ahead and start a blank workbook.

In 2013 and 2016 versions of Excel you will be presented with a blank workbook and one worksheet. In prior versions three worksheets were always presented on startup. You will find most workbooks created prior to 2013 will have two unused worksheets because people forgot to delete them. I'm glad Microsoft did away with that feature because I too was a culprit of not deleting unnecessary worksheets. Let's go over the layout of your first workbook.

Excel Genius - Level 1 - Ledger Path

Introduction to Excel

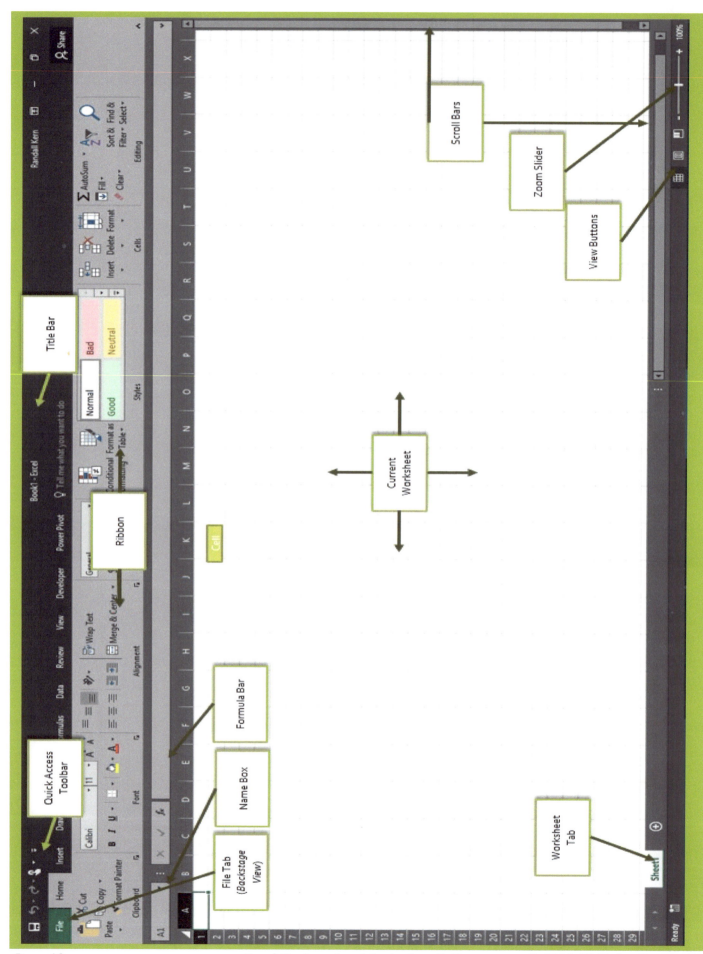

Excel Genius - Level 1 - Ledger Path

- **Title Bar** - The Filename of the Workbook you are working with. By default a new workbook is called Book1. If you open another blank workbook it would be titled Book2.

- **Quick Access Toolbar** - Just what it sounds like. These are buttons that you can quickly click and use. Often Save, Undo, Redo will appear here. You can customize these buttons as well.

- **Ribbon** - This is where the majority of Excel's functionality resides. You should have ribbons for Home, Insert, Page Layout, Formulas, Data, Review and View. We will go over how to add additional ribbons as well as how to customize them in a later course.

- **File Tab/Backstage View** - The File Menu, also called the backstage view, is where you can Save, Create New Workbooks, Open Existing Workbooks, Share, Print, etc. It is also where you can view your account information and explore additional Excel options.

- **Name Box** - The name box is important to note. As you are working with Excel, you may create named ranges for easier access in formulas. These will appear in this box. By default, your current selection appears here (A1 if you haven't clicked anywhere else on the worksheet).

- **Cell** - You notice that Excel is setup with a huge grid. At the top of the grid are letters and to the left of the grid are numbers. Each cell has a name of the letter and the number (look in the name box). We are currently on A1 which can be described as the first column (A) and the first row (1). Hence, Excel names it A1. If you stay on the same row and click in the next column you will be in B1. If you now click on the next row B2.

- **Formula Bar** - As you type in a cell, the formula bar contains the characters you are typing. Actual formula's usually begin with an = sign. Try typing in cell B2 "This Course is Amazing". You will notice that as you complete the sentence there is a flashing curser at the end of the sentence. That means you have not committed that text to the cell. To commit the change, simply hit the Enter key on your keyboard. Excel will shift down to the next row and your text is now added to that cell. Click on the cell again. Notice that the text appears both in the worksheet and in the formula bar. Press the delete key on your keyboard. That clears the data from the cell.

- **Current Worksheet** - The current worksheet is really just a bunch of cells. Excel has 16,384 columns and 1,048,576 rows on each worksheet. Usually this is enough to work with even the most complex data, however; as we will discover later, we can actually analyze many more rows and columns of data.

- **Worksheet Tab** - I've gone over this a bit already. Each workbook opens with a number of tabs (3 in 2010 and prior and 1 in 2013 and after). By default the first sheet is named "Sheet1". You can double click the worksheet and name it almost anything you want.
  View Buttons - The view buttons are just quick access to different types of views. They contain "Normal", "Page Layout", and "Page Break" views. We will discuss each of these and their importance in later discussion, but for now just know they are there.

- **Zoom Slider** - The Zoom Slider is used to zoom in or out of a worksheet. I use this feature rarely, but it is important to note it is there.

- **Scroll Bars** - The scroll bars are used to move up and down and worksheet as well as right and left. In very large datasets you will use these often, but I will offer some shortcuts later that will help you quickly navigate large sets of data without the scrolling.

And there you have it Ladies and Gentlemen. Excel probably doesn't seem so scary anymore. I think it's worth repeating that now you have a blank canvas to create your masterpiece. It's time to pick up our paint brush and get started.

	A
1	A1
2	A2
3	A3
4	A4
5	A5
6	A6

ROWS EXPLAINED

The main grid of Excel is overwhelming to most first time users. There are about 30 rows showing when you start up the program and about 24 columns. I have shown six rows to the left and their names to help break it down. A1 is simply named that because it is the Cell in the first Column (A) of the first Row (1). Columns are Letters, rows are Numbers. It's that easy. A2 is in the First Column (A) and the second Row (2). Usually your first row is reserved to hold the headers for the worksheet. We'll go over this more in the next few chapters. In Excel 2016 there are 1,048,576 rows.

	A	B	C	D	E	F
1	A1	B1	C1	D1	E1	F1
2	A2	B2	C2	D2	E2	F2

COLUMNS EXPLAINED

Columns are as simple as rows. In the above image you see Columns A, B, C, D, E, and F. As you look at the Rows in comparison with the columns you start to see how Excel names them. A1 is in Column A Row 1. F2 is in Column F Row 2. Now there are only 26 letters of the alphabet, so how does Excel deal with that. Well, after Z it introduces a new convention. It starts naming the columns AA,AB, AC, AD etc. After AZ it goes to BA, BB, BC, BD etc. Excel can hold so much data that the last column name (in Excel 2016) in it is XFD. That is 16,384 columns.

Keep in mind that with 16,384 Columns and 1,048,576 rows Excel can handle almost anything. The more data you input, the larger the file. Large Excel files can take an extremely long time to open. There are ways to increase the number of columns and rows Excel can handle, and we will discuss those in a later series. For now, know that you have plenty of room to deal with the data we will be discussing.

Our First Workbook

Our First Workbook

So we begin. I want this series to flow like it does in real life. So, as our learning progresses we will be making changes to our original layout. Each course will build on the same workbook so by the end we will have created a fully functional ledger workbook with dashboard reporting and advanced formulas and functions.

I work in an office environment, and am often asked to create reports and workbooks. I always try to get as much information about what the functionality is before I begin. It never fails that the scope of the project changes midway through my design, or the way I interrogate the data forms more questions. Let me give an example. I was asked to run a report on our call volume for a particular month. I agreed to the project and it was a straightforward idea. I decided to add the data for the company's entire third quarter phone calls on the back end and filter the data for the month in question. I often do things like this in anticipation of further questions. A little caution, adding too much data can make the file incredibly large and draw suspicion from management. Anyway, I reported the data and in one of the charts I put *Third Quarter (May) Inbound Calls by Agent.* After my boss's meeting with the CEO he was indeed asked to report om the entire third quarter. I already had that data, but now he wanted orders by agent added to the report as well. I didn't have that piece in my design, but with some pushing was able to adjust my data model to incorporate it. Still, already having the phone volume was a big time saver.

So to make that story shorter, throughout this series we will have an imaginary boss that constantly changes his mind. His name is Mr. Smith and he is notorious for being indecisive on his projects. As we build our skills he will demand more and more from us, testing our skills with Excel.

 This is Mr. Smith. Whenever you see this icon you will know there is something about to change in your workbook.

Excel Genius - Level 1 - Ledger Path

Mr. Smith just came to our office. He explained his need for a ledger to track his company's financial transactions. He would like to have this project transaction specific so that every transaction he company makes will be recorded in the same worksheet. We ask some basic questions to determine the scope of the project. The questions and the answers appear below:

Q: Is this an internal document or will it be shared with customers, vendors or others?

A: This is an internal document, but we may send it to an auditor or our accountant.

Q: Do you want the workbook to contain data for all of time, or would you like to have a template that we can use monthly, quarterly or yearly?

A: I would like the workbook to be a single workbook that records all of the companies transactions to make it easy to report on any given period.

Q: Do you have a specific color scheme you would like to use?

A: Use our Corporate Colors. (Luckily our company's colors match that of the "Dividend" theme in Microsoft Excel).

Q: What specific columns should be added to the workbook?

A: Date, Pay to / Pay From, Transaction Number, Amount, Category and description. Just create something. I have to get to a meeting.

And with that we begin our blank workbook. It's always a good idea to have the above questions and answers jotted down while you are beginning the creation of the workbook. On large projects I'll often sketch out exactly what I'm thinking so I don't have the limitations of the program in mind. On that note, I will never tell someone something can't be done in Excel. It is a powerful program that has few limitations, and most of those limitations can be overcome by creative thinking.

Workbook Design

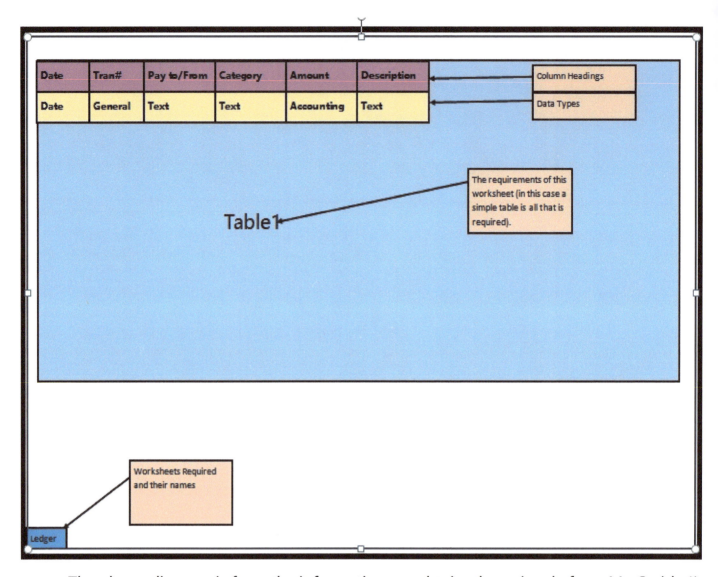

Date	Tran#	Pay to/From	Category	Amount	Description
Date	General	Text	Text	Accounting	Text

Column Headings

Data Types

The requirements of this worksheet (in this case a simple table is all that is required).

Table 1

Worksheets Required and their names

Ledger

The above diagram is from the information we obtained previously from Mr. Smith. I've added nothing additional to this design. Often, I will send this in a quick email for him to review, or schedule a brief 10-20 minute meeting to discuss.

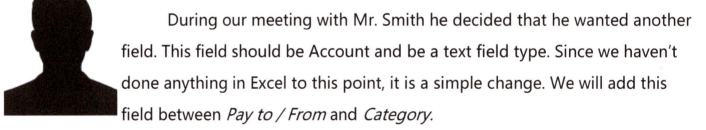

During our meeting with Mr. Smith he decided that he wanted another field. This field should be Account and be a text field type. Since we haven't done anything in Excel to this point, it is a simple change. We will add this field between *Pay to / From* and *Category.*

If you haven't already done so, open a new workbook. Use your Excel shortcut you created earlier or go to your Start Menu and type Excel. Click on the option for Blank Workbook.

Follow these next instructions exactly

1) In Cell A1 type *Date* and press the **TAB** key on your keyboard.

2) In Cell B1 type *Tran #* and press the **TAB** key on your keyboard.

3) In Cell C1 type *Pay To / From* and press the **TAB** key on your keyboard.

4) In Cell D1 type *Account* and press the **TAB** key on your keyboard.

5) In Cell E1 type *Category* and press the **TAB** key on your keyboard.

6) In Cell F1 type *Amount* and press the **TAB** key on your keyboard.

7) In Cell G1 type *Description* and press the **ENTER** key on your keyboard.

You should now be on cell A2. We are going to format each of the entry cells below the headings. There are a number of ways to get to the format cells dialog box in Excel. Pressing **CTRL** and the **1** key at the same time will bring it up and is by far the most efficient way. You can also right click on the Cell and click Format Cells.

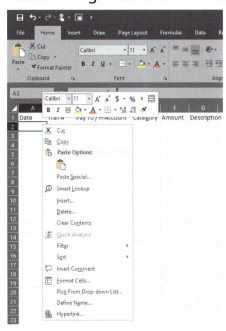

You can also click the arrow box on the Home ribbon in the Number group.

Excel Genius - Level 1 - Ledger Path

Any way you choose to do this is fine, I prefer keyboard shortcuts wherever possible. You should see the Format dialog box at this point.

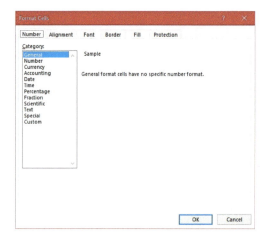

Since Cell A2 is a date field, we need to assign it as such. Click on date in the Number section of the Format Dialog Box. I prefer my fields to all align when I'm creating a workbook, so I will choose the MM/DD/YY type. You can choose any date type you would like.

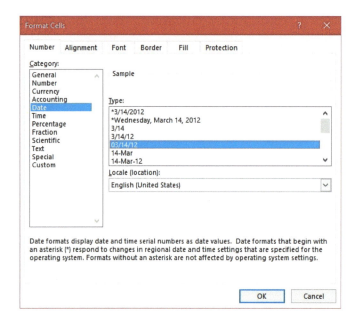

Once you've chosen yours simply press OK. Now press **Tab** to go to cell B2.

Since General is the default type for a cell we can skip cell B2. Simply press **TAB on your** keyboard. Now we are at cell C2.

The Pay To / From field will be a text field. It will be a person or a company. Go to the Format Dialog with the instructions from the previous page for this cell. Click on Text and press OK. Press the **TAB** key to go to cell D2.

The Account field will be text as well. Once you've changed that field type, press **TAB** to go to cell E2.

The Category field will be text as well. Once you've entered that field type press **TAB** to go to cell F2.

The Amount field will be an Accounting type. Again, go to format cells and this time click on Accounting. You will be given options for Decimal Places (choose 2) and Symbol (choose your currency symbol). Press OK and then press **TAB** to go to the last field, cell G2.

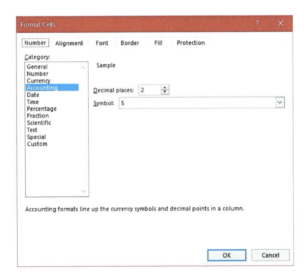

Creating Tables

The last field, Description, will be a long text type. Change the format of the cell to Text. Then, on the Home Ribbon, click on Wrap Text.

Ok, the hard part is over. Now, using some of our Excel Magic, we are going to convert these fields to a table. A little background on tables first. The reason we want to make this a table is to hold the field types we just created for any new rows added. So as we add transactions, the row we add them on will maintain the same field types as the row above it. Also, tables are incredibly easy to reference in formulas and functions and provide unique names to each of the columns, as well as the table itself. Pay attention to the image above. There are tabs on this ribbon for: File, Insert, Draw, Page Layout, Formulas, Data, Review, View and Developer. We are going to navigate to the Insert Tab to create the table. Once you click that your screen show look similar to the below image:

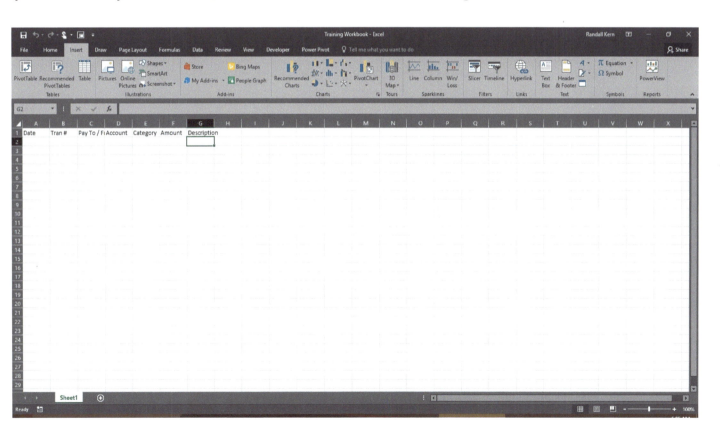

Excel Genius - Level 1 - Ledger Path

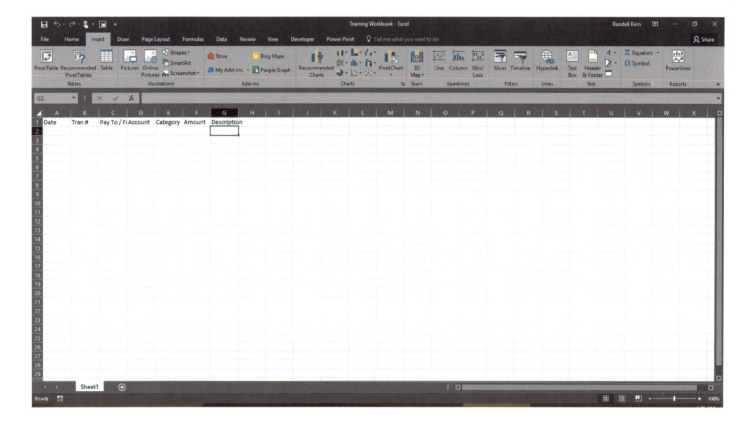

So now we need to select where we want to put the table. Starting with Cell A1, Click and Drag with your mouse to cell G2 and let go of the mouse button. You should have selected everything we worked with up to this point.

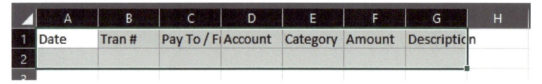

Now, on the Insert Tab on the Ribbon click Table. A dialog box will pop up and show you some options. The *Where is the data for your table?* Field should read something that looks a little Greek. It should read exactly as follows *=$A$1:$G$2*. This is important as it is referencing a cell range. We will go over this more in detail as we discover formulas. Make sure that the box for *My table has headers* is checked, then press OK.

Excel Genius - Level 1 - Ledger Path

You should now be presented with a beautiful table in your worksheet. Notice the top row has changed color, the second row is a light blue, and the column widths have adjusted to fit the text we entered on row 1. Row 1 will now be referred to as our heading row and will play a major role in our formulas and calculations later. Row 2 has held all of our formats that we previously assigned. If you don't believe me, click on the cells and open the Format dialog as we discussed previously.

Now for some tidying up. Remember, that Mr. Smith wanted our Color Scheme to stay in line with the company's color scheme. We discovered earlier that theme was equal to Dividend in Excel. To change this, we will go to the Ribbon and select the Page Layout tab.

Click on the Themes drop down arrow and select Dividend. You will see that the colors have changed on your table immediately. You have just performed your second magic trick.

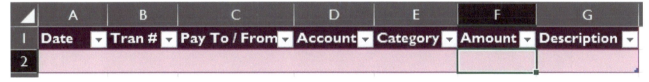

Also notice that in the ribbon you have a new tab of Design. Just above design it has the words Table Tools (if you don't see it click on one of the cells in the new table). Click on that tab and let's explore a couple options.

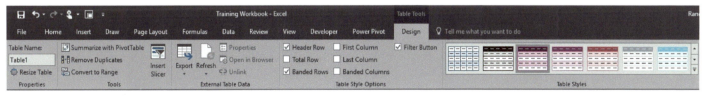

Excel Genius - Level 1 - Ledger Path

Naming Worksheets and Tables

Excel Genius - Level 1 - Ledger Path

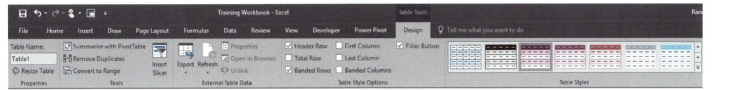

On the left of the menu you should see an option for Table Name. In it, you will see the words Table1. Notice there is no space between Table and 1. This is important, because Excel has a hard time recognizing spaces when you are writing formulas. Let's select that text and rename it as *AcctLedger*. This will be easier to remember as we move on through the course and begin writing formulas.

Now we are going rename the worksheet as well. We want this to be a little different then the name of the table, so we will simply name it Ledger. On the lower left side of the screen you will see a worksheet title of Sheet1 (again following the pattern of No Spaces). We are going to change that to *Ledger*.

To do this, use your mouse to double click on the words Sheet1. You will see the text highlight. Now, simply type *Ledger* over that text and press Enter. You should see the change below.

We are going to do one more formatting change. We are going to change some of the column widths to account for the data that will be entered into them. To show you how Excel deals with data I offer you the following two examples.

Setting Column Width

Excel Genius - Level 1 - Ledger Path

In the above example, I have entered a lot of text into cell B2. Since there is no data in the same row for Columns B, C, D, E, F and G; Excel shows the text as it was entered. If we add text to column C in the same row, Excel will shorten the displayed text to the beginning of that Column.

The data in B2 hasn't changed, just what is displayed on your screen has. If you select cell B2, you will see the entire contents of that cell in the formula bar.

So, we know that some of this data will be longer than others. We can adjust the column widths to account for that. For the following fields you will click the letter in the column provided, right click on the letter, then select Column Width. This will bring up a dialog box.

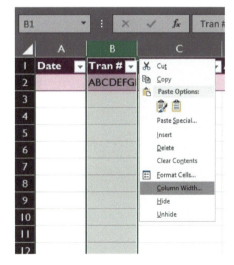

Excel Genius - Level 1 - Ledger Path

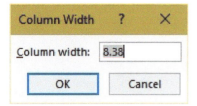

We will just fill in the desired column width. Change the widths of the following columns:

Column	Field Name	Column Width
B	Tran #	13
C	Pay To / From	25
D	Account	13
E	Category	25
F	Amount	12
G	Description	60

Now your worksheet should look similar to this

Of course the above numbers are just a guess of how long the fields can be. These can be adjusted as you are using the workbook since the width has little effect on anything but the display.

Uh Oh, it's Mr. Smith again. He wanted to make sure you knew that the category field should only contain category's that exist within your company. Luckily, he brought you a list of them so you don't have to hope you remember them all.

Excel Genius - Level 1 - Ledger Path

Saving Workbooks

Let's first save our work to this point. You should save your work periodically, in case you get distracted. Even the best of us have closed a workbook and said no when it asks if you want to save your changes. It is heartbreaking every time. To save you have a couple options. We are going to explore the basic save function. There are a few different ways to access this. The first time you save a workbook, even with the basic save command, it will prompt you to use the Save As command. The basic save command is limited to an already existing workbook. It simply saves your progress to a certain point. Since there is no workbook generated, Save will ask you to determine where you want to put the file.

Here are the different options for Save:

1) CTRL + S on your keyboard
2) File Menu on the Ribbon and option Save
3) Quick Access Toolbar Save button (if you hover over the buttons they will describe what they do, by default this button is included in the toolbar.

No matter which option you use, it will take you to the File Menu or Backstage View with the Save As option active.

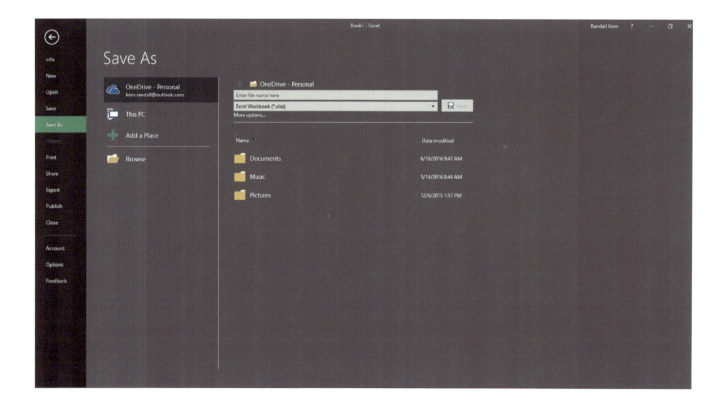

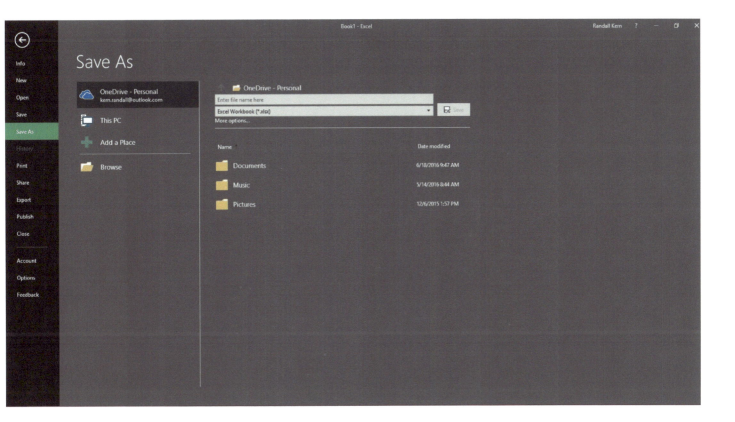

Now we need to chose where to save the file. Three options are available (actually four but we will only explore three for now).

1) One Drive - If you have a Microsoft Office 365 subscription, you probably have some type of plan for One Drive included. Check with your provider to see how much disk space you have. This saves your workbook to the cloud and makes it accessible to any computer you use that has an internet connection.

2) This PC - This will default to your DOCUMENTS folder on your computer. Most people use this option and perhaps will create a folder to contain the workbook in.

3) Browse - By Far my favorite option, perhaps because I am old school. This brings up the familiar SAVE AS dialog box that Microsoft is known for. Whenever we use the SAVE AS command I will be using this option.

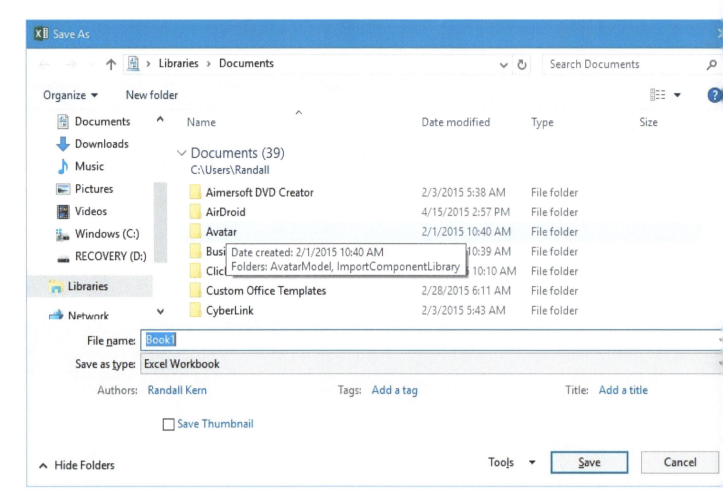

When you use the BROWSE Command there are 3 main areas to the dialog box. To the left you see a list of your folders and areas on your computer or network. To the right you have a specific folder that is your default folder (In this case DOCUMENTS). And underneath all of that you have FILE NAME and SAVE AS TYPE. Note that if you are using EXCEL 2016 some features may not be compatible with users on a previous version of EXCEL. Let's say you have EXCEL 2016 but many others in your office are using EXCEL 2003. You would use the SAVE AS TYPE of EXCEL 97-2003. This would remove any features that wouldn't be compatible with those version. For now, we will assume everyone in the office is on EXCEL 2016 and use the default SAVE AS TYPE of EXCEL WORKBOOK. On the left menu choose a location where you will be able to easily find the workbook (preferably desktop). Type in a FILE NAME that makes sense, such as Ledger and press the OK button. Your progress has now been saved.

Adding New Worksheets

Excel Genius - Level 1 - Ledger Path

Back to Mr. Smith's newest addition to our work book. The below document is what he handed to you:

SMITH'S MARKET CATEGORIES		
CATEGORY	DESCRIPTION	CREDIT OR DEBIT
COST OF GOODS	ITEMS PURCHASED FOR RESALE	DEBIT
SALARIES AND WAGES	EMPLOYEE WAGES	DEBIT
RENT AND UTILITIES	RENT PAID OR UTILITIES PAID	DEBIT
OTHER EXPENSES	ANY OTHER EXPENSES	DEBIT
RECEIVABLES	MONEY PAID BY CUSTOMERS	CREDIT
INTEREST AND DIVIDENDS	BANK INTEREST	CREDIT
OTHER INCOME	ANY OTHER INCOME	CREDIT

So now we will add a new worksheet to put these categories into. We will add all of the above columns to the new worksheet and create another table. Begin by adding a new worksheet. At the bottom of the current worksheet, where the tab shows *Ledger*, click the + button.

You will get a new worksheet labeled *Sheet1*. Double click *Sheet1* to change the label to *Categories*. Now, in Cell A1 on the worksheet *Categories*, type *Category*. In Cell B1 type *Description*. In Cell C1 type *Credit/Debit*. Your worksheet should look similar to the one below.

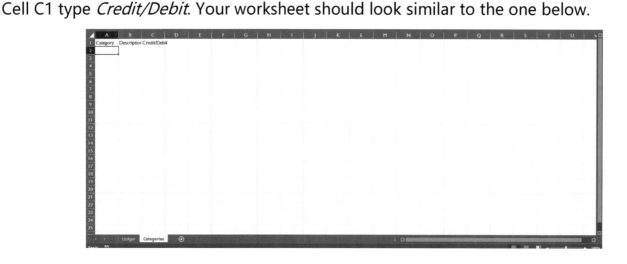

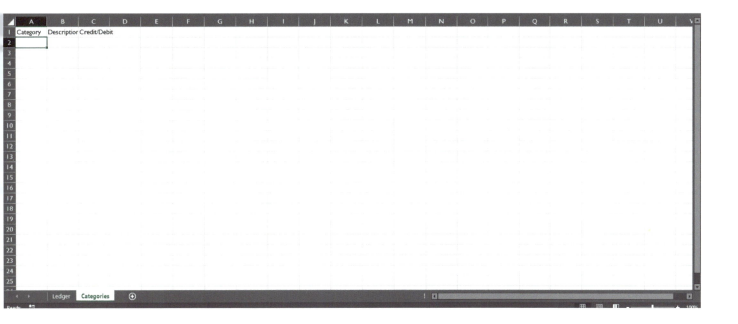

Since all of the fields will be a format type of TEXT we will select Cells A2-C2. To do this, Left Click on cell A2 and with the button held down, drag the mouse to the right until cells A2, B2 and C2 are highlighted.

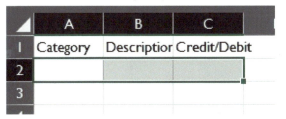

Now, Right Click on cell A2 and choose the menu for FORMAT CELLS (you can also press your CTRL + 1 keys on your keyboard as a shortcut). From the Format dialog box choose TEXT and press OK.

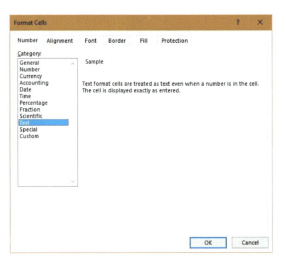

Excel Genius - Level 1 - Ledger Path

Now we can create our *Category* Table. To Do this we will select Cells A1 - C2. With your mouse, left click on cell A1 and keeping the left button held, drag your cursor to cell C2. You should have the entire contents of this table selected.

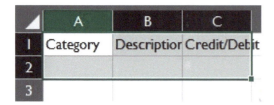

Now click on the INSERT tab on the ribbon.

Click on the Table option in the Tables group. The dialog should look familiar.

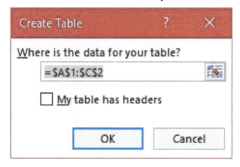

Remember to check the box for MY TABLE HAS HEADERS, and then press OK. You should now have a new Table in your workbook on your *Categories* worksheet. After a little tidying up we can start entering some data.

Using the methods discussed on page 22 extend the columns to the following widths:

Column	Field Name	Column Width
A	Category	25
B	Description	25
C	Credit/Debit	25

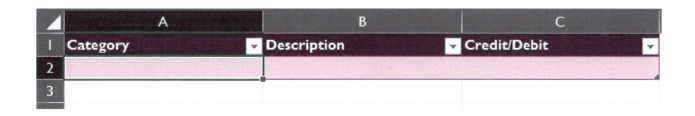

Our worksheet is starting to look Beautiful. Let's give this table a meaningful name. We'll call it Category (see page 20 if you can't remember how to name the table). Now we can enter the data into the *Category* Table on the *Categories* worksheet. We will start at cell A2 and enter the first row of the data below (Enter in ALL CAPITAL LETTERS).

SMITH'S MARKET CATEGORIES		
CATEGORY	DESCRIPTION	CREDIT OR DEBIT
COST OF GOODS	ITEMS PURCHASED FOR RESALE	DEBIT
SALARIES AND WAGES	EMPLOYEE WAGES	DEBIT
RENT AND UTILITIES	RENT PAID OR UTILITIES PAID	DEBIT
OTHER EXPENSES	ANY OTHER EXPENSES	DEBIT
RECEIVABLES	MONEY PAID BY CUSTOMERS	CREDIT
INTEREST AND DIVIDENDS	BANK INTEREST	CREDIT
OTHER INCOME	ANY OTHER INCOME	CREDIT

Once this data has been entered, make sure you are in Cell C2 and press the **TAB** key on your keyboard. You should now have a second row to enter data into (row3).

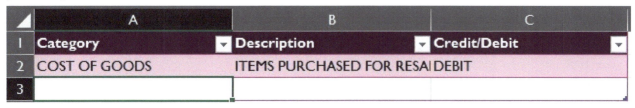

Enter the rest of the data, pressing the **TAB** key on your keyboard in Column C after entering that rows data.

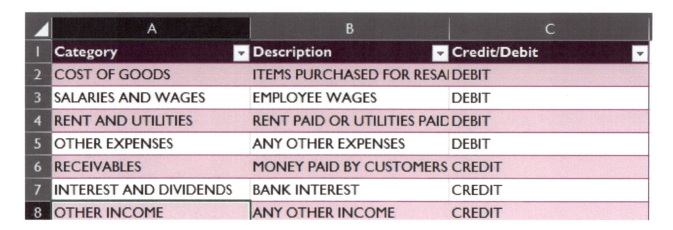

Category	Description	Credit/Debit
COST OF GOODS	ITEMS PURCHASED FOR RESAI	DEBIT
SALARIES AND WAGES	EMPLOYEE WAGES	DEBIT
RENT AND UTILITIES	RENT PAID OR UTILITIES PAID	DEBIT
OTHER EXPENSES	ANY OTHER EXPENSES	DEBIT
RECEIVABLES	MONEY PAID BY CUSTOMERS	CREDIT
INTEREST AND DIVIDENDS	BANK INTEREST	CREDIT
OTHER INCOME	ANY OTHER INCOME	CREDIT

This is how your table should look. Notice how some of the wording in the Description field is cut off. We can automatically resize the field using one of Excel's best tricks. On your *Categories* worksheet, double click the line in between Column B & C.

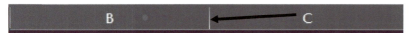

Now you should be able to see all of the text in the *Description* column.

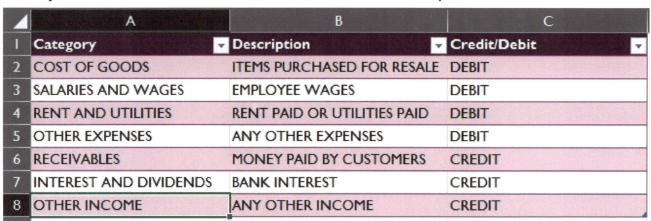

Category	Description	Credit/Debit
COST OF GOODS	ITEMS PURCHASED FOR RESALE	DEBIT
SALARIES AND WAGES	EMPLOYEE WAGES	DEBIT
RENT AND UTILITIES	RENT PAID OR UTILITIES PAID	DEBIT
OTHER EXPENSES	ANY OTHER EXPENSES	DEBIT
RECEIVABLES	MONEY PAID BY CUSTOMERS	CREDIT
INTEREST AND DIVIDENDS	BANK INTEREST	CREDIT
OTHER INCOME	ANY OTHER INCOME	CREDIT

We have our first complete table. As our company grows, we may need to add additional categories. This is done by simply going to the last row (currently row 8), going to the last column (currently column C), clicking on Cell C8, and pressing **TAB** on your keyboard. This entire table, and any future changes, will help us validate the data on our *Ledger* worksheet.

Excel Genius - Level 1 - Ledger Path

Naming Ranges

We are now going to make the CATEGORY column accessible in a formula. We will be introducing the NAME MANAGER. Let's take a look at what Microsoft has to say about the Name Manager:

> By using names, you can make your formulas much easier to understand and maintain. You can define a name for a cell range, function, constant, or table. Once you adopt the practice of using names in your workbook, you can easily update, audit, and manage these names.

So, in order to quickly reference our CATEGORY column in DATA VALIDATION, we are going to name it CATEGORIES. It sounds redundant, and it is, but from then on when we want to use that column in a formula we can simply type CATEGORIES and Excel will know what we mean.

1) Select Cells A2 through A8 (Left click on A2 and hold the button, drag down to A8)

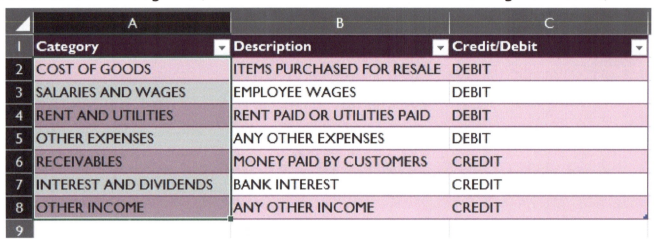

	A	B	C
1	Category	Description	Credit/Debit
2	COST OF GOODS	ITEMS PURCHASED FOR RESALE	DEBIT
3	SALARIES AND WAGES	EMPLOYEE WAGES	DEBIT
4	RENT AND UTILITIES	RENT PAID OR UTILITIES PAID	DEBIT
5	OTHER EXPENSES	ANY OTHER EXPENSES	DEBIT
6	RECEIVABLES	MONEY PAID BY CUSTOMERS	CREDIT
7	INTEREST AND DIVIDENDS	BANK INTEREST	CREDIT
8	OTHER INCOME	ANY OTHER INCOME	CREDIT
9			

2) On the Ribbon, choose the Formulas Tab

3) Click on Name Manager

4) Click on New

5) Notice the NAME is COST_OF_GOODS. Excel hates spaces so puts the "_" in place of a space. We want to change this name to CATEGORIES. Simply press OK and close the NAME MANAGER.

You now have a named range. Remember, if we add or remove categories to the Category table, they will be included with our data validation.

Excel Genius - Level 1 - Ledger Path

Data Validation

Excel Genius - Level 1 - Ledger Path

Data Validation is used in Excel in a number of ways, when you want to limit the data that is entered to a cell. Since we are using tables on our worksheets, any data validation we create within the first table row, will be applied when we add additional table rows. So let's start our first validation rule.

> *Data validation is an Excel feature that you can use to define restrictions on what data can or should be entered in a cell. You can configure data validation to prevent users from entering data that is not valid.*

1) Click on the *Ledger* worksheet and click on Cell E2 (the row under the *Category* label).
2) On the Ribbon, choose the DATA tab

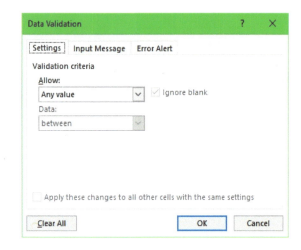

3) Click on the drop down in the Group DATA TESTS on the icon DATA VALIDATION.
4) Click on DATA VALIDATION (if you click the actual icon it is a shortcut to the DATA VALIDATION dialog box).
5) Under VALIDATION CRITERIA ALLOW: click the drop down for ANY VALUE
6) Choose LIST

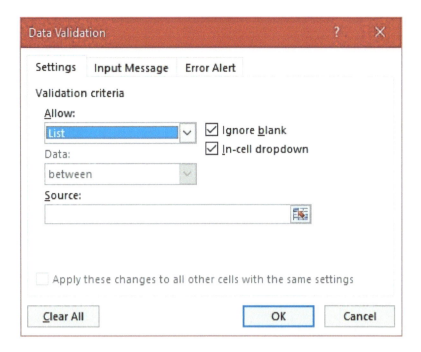

Notice the options have changed. We will always use the Ignore Blank and In-Cell Dropdown check boxes. The Ignore Blank does not validate the data if there is nothing there. If you want to require a value, you can click the *X* to remove it. The In-Cell dropdown provides a dropdown menu that lists all available options. If you know the option you can type it in the cell, or choose it from the dropdown menu. Note that by typing the data, you must match the case of the text in the list.

7) Click in the box under SOURCE.

8) Type in the source box *=Categories*. This tells Excel we want to use that named range we created previously. Press OK and your data validation is done.

Your Category cell (E2) should now contain a drop down arrow when you select it. If you click the dropdown, you will see all of the items from your Category table.

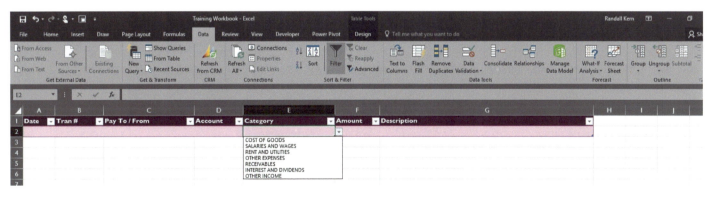

Mr. Smith just stopped by your office to see your progress. He is impressed with your Data Validation on the category field. There are a couple additional requirements he thought of when you showed him this. He would like you to create a validation rule for Account using the Account Sheet below. He would also like, on the *Category* worksheet, and the *Accounts* worksheet you will be adding, a column for Total Amount, which will sum the totals from the *Ledger* worksheet for each CATEGORY and ACCOUNT. He has also provided us with a copy of the current month's ledger to put in our worksheet. Thanks Mr. Smith, more work.

SMITH'S MARKET ACCOUNTS	
ACCOUNT	DESCRIPTION
OPERATING CHECKING	FOR OPERATING COSTS
PAYROLL CHECKING	FOR PAYROLL

SMITH'S MARKET LEDGER						
DATE	TRAN #	PAY TO/FROM	ACCOUNT	CATEGORY	AMOUNT	DESCRIPTION
06/04	001	WALLEY MART	OPERATING	COST OF GOODS	1,436.00	GOODS
06/04		TRANSACTIONS	OPERATING	RECEIVABLES	8,757.55	REVENUE
06/05	002	PAYROLL	PAYROLL	SALARIES AND WAGES	2,187.63	PAYROLL
06/05		TRANSACTIONS	OPERATING	RECEIVABLES	10,457.80	REVENUE
06/06		TRANSACTIONS	OPERATING	RECEIVABLES	10,457.80	REVENUE
06/07		TRANSACTIONS	OPERATING	RECEIVABLES	10,457.80	REVENUE
06/08		TRANSACTIONS	OPERATING	RECEIVABLES	10,457.80	REVENUE
06/08	003	RENT	OPERATING	RENT AND UTILITIES	980.00	RENT
06/08	004	VENDING CORP	OPERATING	OTHER EXPENSES	157.60	VENDING COSTS

Excel Genius - Level 1 - Ledger Path

Let's start by entering the data Mr. Smith gave us. We'll enter the first line of data.

	Date	Tran #	Pay To / From	Account	Category	Amount	Description
2	4-Jun	001	WALLEY MART	OPERATING	COST OF GOODS	1,436.00	GOODS

Remember, to add a new row to a table you must be at the last column in the last row (currently G2). Press **TAB** on your keyboard to add the new row.

	Date	Tran #	Pay To / From	Account	Category	Amount	Description
2	06/04/16	001	WALLEY MART	OPERATING	COST OF GOODS	1,436.00	GOODS
3							

Continue entering the data, remembering to press **TAB** on your keyboard at the end of each row to insert another row. Your finished table should look like this:

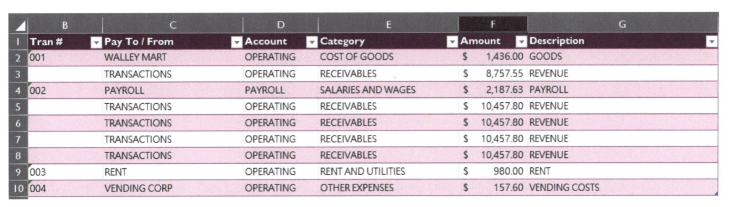

	Tran #	Pay To / From	Account	Category	Amount	Description
2	001	WALLEY MART	OPERATING	COST OF GOODS	$ 1,436.00	GOODS
3		TRANSACTIONS	OPERATING	RECEIVABLES	$ 8,757.55	REVENUE
4	002	PAYROLL	PAYROLL	SALARIES AND WAGES	$ 2,187.63	PAYROLL
5		TRANSACTIONS	OPERATING	RECEIVABLES	$ 10,457.80	REVENUE
6		TRANSACTIONS	OPERATING	RECEIVABLES	$ 10,457.80	REVENUE
7		TRANSACTIONS	OPERATING	RECEIVABLES	$ 10,457.80	REVENUE
8		TRANSACTIONS	OPERATING	RECEIVABLES	$ 10,457.80	REVENUE
9	003	RENT	OPERATING	RENT AND UTILITIES	$ 980.00	RENT
10	004	VENDING CORP	OPERATING	OTHER EXPENSES	$ 157.60	VENDING COSTS

Notice that there are positive values for expenses. This doesn't really make sense as they should be negative numbers. I'm going to show you a quick trick to turn a positive number into a negative number. First, we are going to enter –1 in Cell F12.

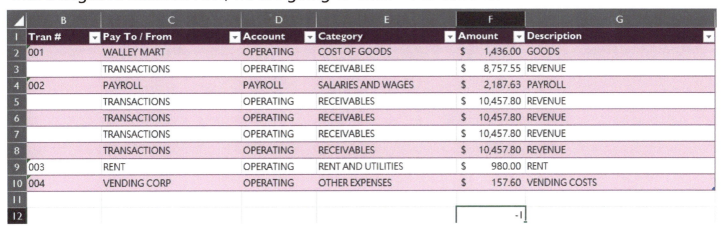

	Tran #	Pay To / From	Account	Category	Amount	Description
2	001	WALLEY MART	OPERATING	COST OF GOODS	$ 1,436.00	GOODS
3		TRANSACTIONS	OPERATING	RECEIVABLES	$ 8,757.55	REVENUE
4	002	PAYROLL	PAYROLL	SALARIES AND WAGES	$ 2,187.63	PAYROLL
5		TRANSACTIONS	OPERATING	RECEIVABLES	$ 10,457.80	REVENUE
6		TRANSACTIONS	OPERATING	RECEIVABLES	$ 10,457.80	REVENUE
7		TRANSACTIONS	OPERATING	RECEIVABLES	$ 10,457.80	REVENUE
8		TRANSACTIONS	OPERATING	RECEIVABLES	$ 10,457.80	REVENUE
9	003	RENT	OPERATING	RENT AND UTILITIES	$ 980.00	RENT
10	004	VENDING CORP	OPERATING	OTHER EXPENSES	$ 157.60	VENDING COSTS
11						
12					-1	

Making Positive Values Negative Values

Now we are going to select all of the cells that should be negative as well as the –1 we just entered. To do this we will select the –1 in Cell F12. Right click the mouse and choose Copy. Press and hold the **CTRL** key on your keyboard and click cells F2, F4, F9, and F10.

Tran #	Pay To / From	Account	Category	Amount	Description
001	WALLEY MART	OPERATING	COST OF GOODS	$ 1,436.00	GOODS
	TRANSACTIONS	OPERATING	RECEIVABLES	$ 8,757.55	REVENUE
002	PAYROLL	PAYROLL	SALARIES AND WAGES	$ 2,187.63	PAYROLL
	TRANSACTIONS	OPERATING	RECEIVABLES	$ 10,457.80	REVENUE
	TRANSACTIONS	OPERATING	RECEIVABLES	$ 10,457.80	REVENUE
	TRANSACTIONS	OPERATING	RECEIVABLES	$ 10,457.80	REVENUE
	TRANSACTIONS	OPERATING	RECEIVABLES	$ 10,457.80	REVENUE
003	RENT	OPERATING	RENT AND UTILITIES	$ 980.00	RENT
004	VENDING CORP	OPERATING	OTHER EXPENSES	$ 157.60	VENDING COSTS
				-1	

Now, release the **CTRL** key and right click on Cell F12. Choose the option for Paste Special which will bring up a dialog box. Under Paste you will choose VALUES. Under Operation you will choose Multiply.

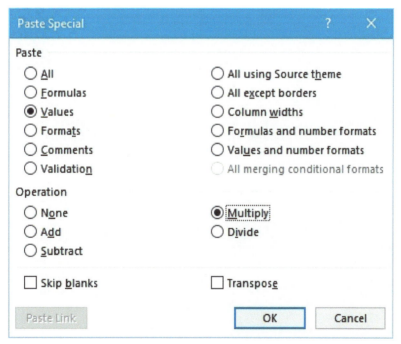

Press the OK button and all of your values you selected are now negative. You can delete the –1 in Cell F12 by clicking on it and pressing the **DELETE** key on your keyboard. Perfect, our ledger is now complete for the month. Let's finish up the *Categories* worksheet by adding the column that Mr. Smith asked us for.

Time for some really impressive formula writing.

Formula Writing (SUMIF)

Excel Genius - Level 1 - Ledger Path

Let's get to the *Categories* worksheet. Click on the Categories tab to open it. In Cell D1 we're going to type Total Amount. Notice, Excel automatically creates a new column with blank cells for the number of rows that exists in your table. We will need to take a look at the formatting of these cells though, as any new column inherits the column to the lefts format. Select Cells D2 through D8. Open the Format Cells dialog box (**CTRL+1** on your keyboard, or right click and choose the option for Format Cells).

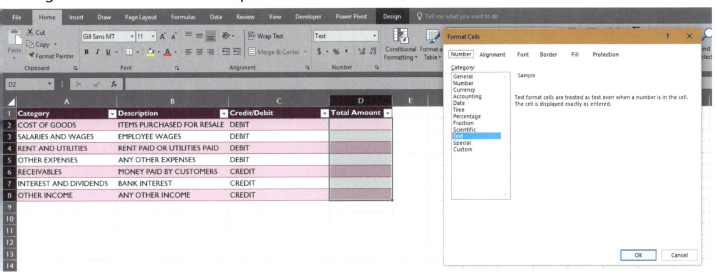

Notice that Text is already highlighted. We want this to be an Accounting format with the decimal places set to 2 and the symbol set to $. Once these have been selected, press OK.

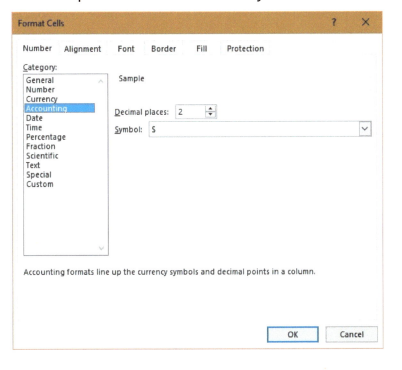

Now for the actual formula writing. Keep in mind that we already setup the name Categories in the name manager as we write this. We are going to use the SUMIF formula. Here is Microsoft's explanation of that:

You use the SUMIF function to sum the values in a range that meet criteria that you specify.

Every Formula contains a Function and every function has a Syntax. A Syntax is simply the layout of the function and its arguments. Let's look at the SUMIF Function's syntax:

=SUMIF(range, criteria, [sum_range])

The next portion is simply explaining what we're going to do, we will walk through it step by step on the next few pages.

Every formula should start with an = sign. This simply tells Excel we want to write a formula. Next we type the Function that we want to use (in this case SUMIF. We begin the function by typing an open parentheses "(". So now we have

=SUMIF(. Next is the really fun part. To begin we need to click on the *Ledger* worksheet. Then we will select Cells C2 through C10 (the Category Columns contents). After we have that in place we need to add a comma "," to tell the Formula that we are ready to move to the Criteria argument. For the criteria, we will simply type CATEGORIES and then place a "," after that. This is where we are referring to that named range we created. By typing that, we are looking at the current row we are typing into, Row 2, and the Category in that field (COST OF GOODS). What range do we want to look at? Now in this example we want to look at our *Ledger* worksheet in the Category column. Notice that Sum Range is is brackets. This means that it is an optional part of the Formula. In this case, if we omit it, we will get 0's because the Criteria portion is text and we are using a sum function. So for our Sum Range portion we want the Value of Amount on the *Ledger* worksheet. On the *Ledger* worksheet select Cells F2 through F10. We will close the Formula once we write this with a ")" and press enter to commit the change. Once we have finished the formula, since we are working on a table; our formula will be added to every row in the table, with the Criteria changing to match the value in that row.

NOW - Let's run through this

DO NOT USE SPACES IN ANY OF THE FOLLOWING STEPS. I am writing out the formula below so you can see how it looks. Follow the instructions, rather than simply typing it so you know how we achieve it.

=SUMIF(AcctLedger[Category],Categories,AcctLedger[Amount])

1) In Cell D2, on the *Categories* worksheet, type *=SUMIF(* *this* starts our Formula

2) Click on the *Ledger* worksheet

3) Select Cells E2 through E10

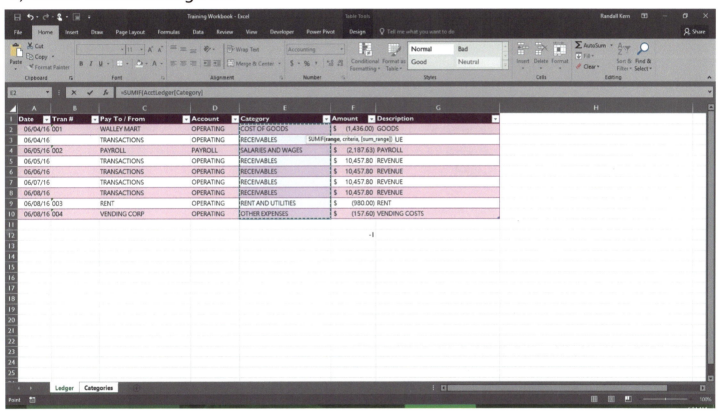

4) Press the "," key on your keyboard to move to the Criteria part of the formula.

5) Type Categories (the named range we created) and press the "," key on your keyboard.

6) On the *Ledger* worksheet select Cells F2 through F10 (the Amount contents)

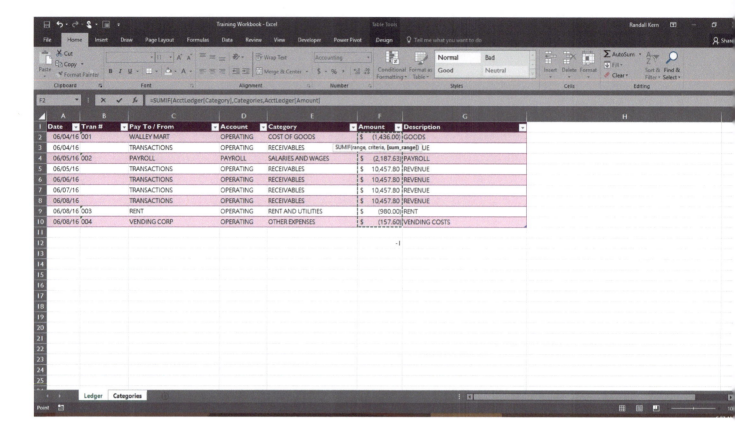

7) Press the ")" on your keyboard.

8) Press Enter to commit the changes

Your table should now have amounts in all of the rows on the *Categories* worksheet under the TOTAL AMOUNT column (Column D). You just wrote your very first formula. Congratulations.

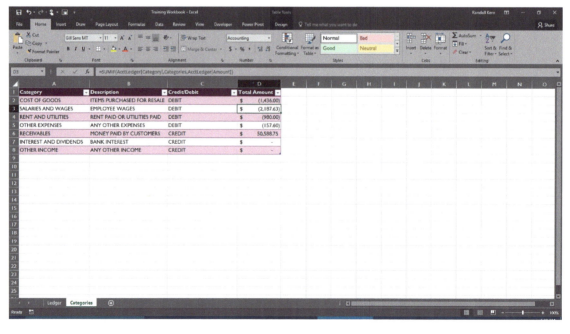

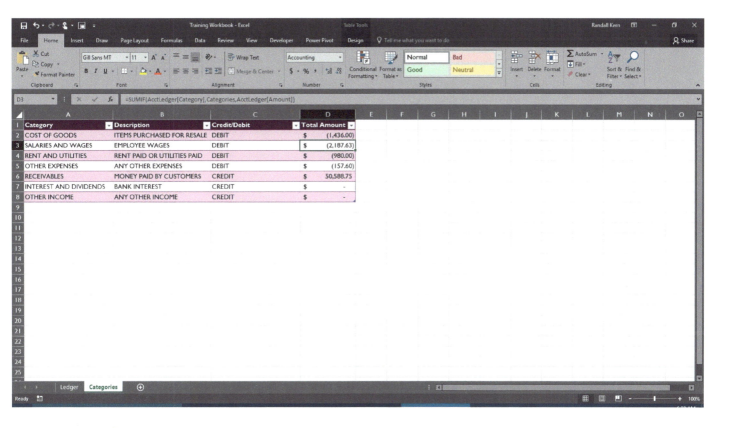

Now I want you to pay attention to the TOTAL AMOUNT for the Category OTHER INCOME (Cell D8). Notice that it is $- which is the accounting format for $0.00. Click on the *Ledger* worksheet. In cell A11 type 06/09/16. Press **TAB**. Press **TAB** to skip Column B, the TRAN # column. Type VENDING CORP in Cell C11, PAY TO/FROM. On your keyboard HOLD DOWN the **CTRL** and **SHIFT** keys. While holding those keys press the " key. This copy's the data from the above line (this way you don't have to type it again). You can also begin typing VENDING CORP and Excel will recognize it). Once you have VENDING CORP in cell C11, press **TAB** on your keyboard. For account type OPERATING and press **TAB.** Under the Category Heading we are going to type OTHER INCOME. Remember, this is our Data Validation field so it must be typed in UPPER CASE. Data validation fields are case sensitive. You can also click the dropdown and select OTHER INCOME. Press the **TAB** key. Under AMOUNT type 281.75. This is the amount we received from VENDING CORP, so the amount will be a positive number. Press **TAB**. Under DESCRIPTION type VENDING INCOME. Press Enter. Now click on your *Categories* worksheet. You should see that OTHER INCOME has changed to $281.75. Our formula is working correctly.

　　　　　Excel Genius - Level 1 - Ledger Path

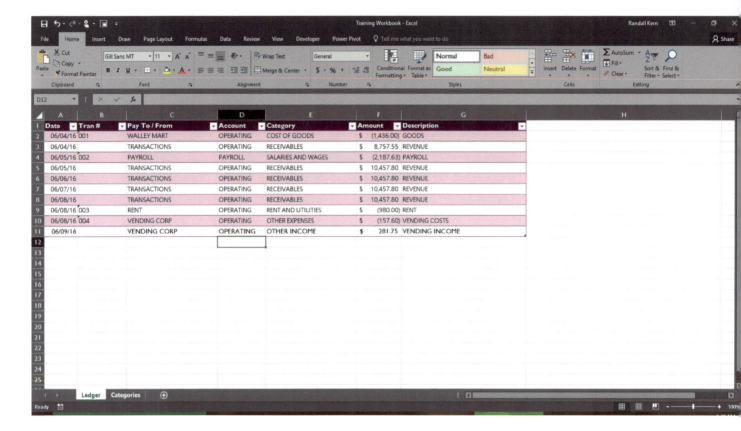

Above is our *Ledger* Worksheet.

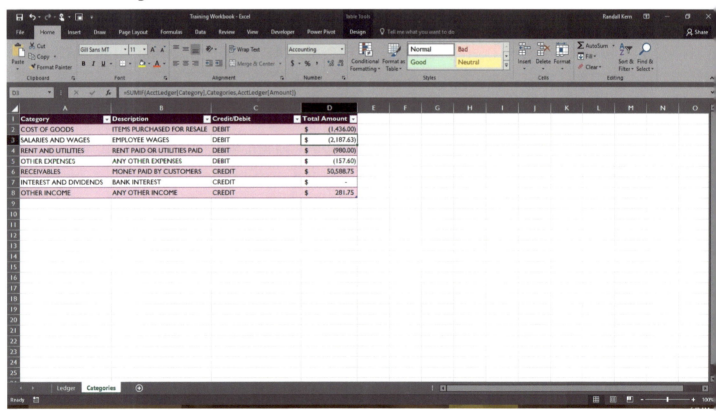

Above is our *Categories* worksheet.

Copying Worksheets

Excel Genius - Level 1 - Ledger Path

We only have one more requirement for this project. Mr. Smith asked us to include another worksheet for ACCOUNTS. We will use this Worksheet for data validation into the ACCOUNT column in the *Ledger* worksheet. Since the *Accounts* worksheet will have the same basic functionality as the *Categories* worksheet, we will simply duplicate *Categories*.

To copy a worksheet, simply right click on any worksheet tab (either *Ledger* or *Categories* in this case).

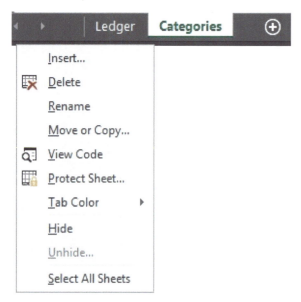

We will then select MOVE OR COPY...

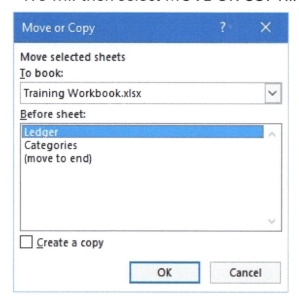

Excel Genius - Level 1 - Ledger Path

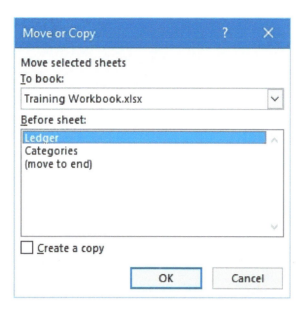

Now we will click on the *Categories* worksheet in the Before Sheet section of the dialog box.

Make sure that Create a copy is checked and then press OK.

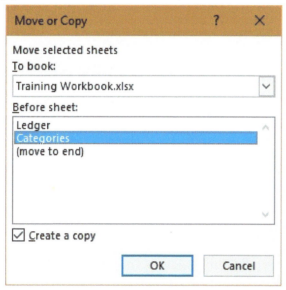

You should now see another worksheet named *Categories (2)*. Notice that it made an exact duplicate with all of our data and formulas in it.

Now to finish up the workbook we just need to make this worksheet the *Accounts* worksheet and finalize our workbook.

First we will rename the worksheet. Double click on the *Categories (2)* worksheet and rename it to *Accounts*.

Click on Cell A1 and change the heading from Category to Account. All of the other headings make sense, except Credit/Debit. Each account will have Credits and Debits. We will delete that column. To do this right click on cell C1 Credit/Debit.

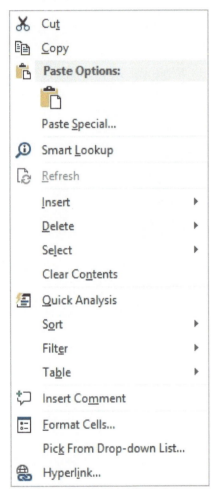

Select Delete, then select Table Columns.

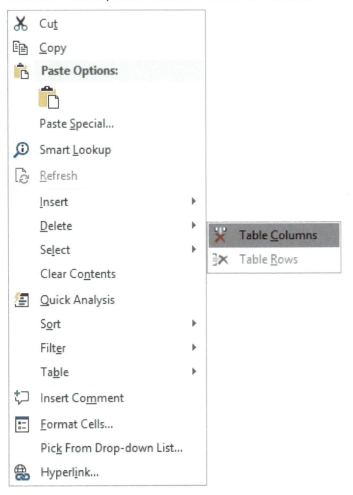

Here is how your workbook should look now:

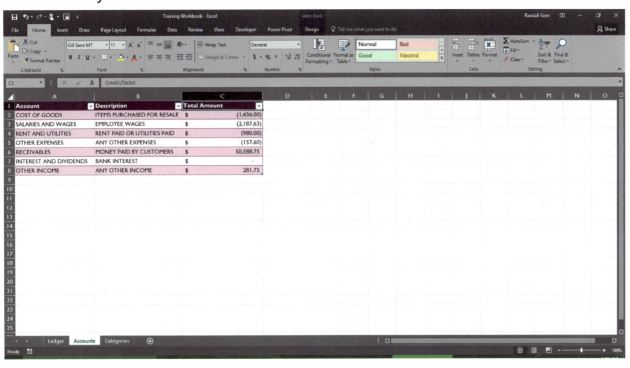

Excel Genius - Level 1 - Ledger Path

Next select any cell in the table (Cells A1 through C8). Click on the DESIGN tab on the Ribbon.

Notice that the TABLE NAME has been renamed to Category4 in the PROPERTIES group of the Design Ribbon. That doesn't make sense. Highlight the text Category4 and rename it to Accts, then press **ENTER** on your keyboard to commit the change. Outstanding, our work is almost done here. All of our data on the *Accounts* sheet has been duplicated from the *Categories* sheet and isn't relevant to the current table.

We are going to delete all of the rows except the first row, because it contains the formula we will want to modify to show the balance of each account. To delete the other rows, simply select cells A3 through A8 (Left click on Cell A3 and while holding the left button drag your mouse down to cell A8).

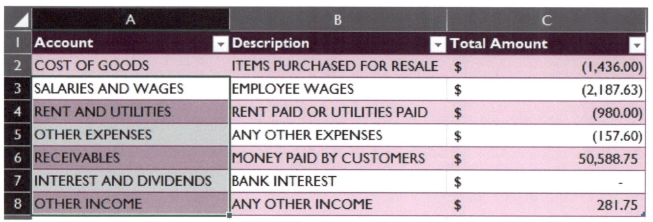

Account	Description	Total Amount
COST OF GOODS	ITEMS PURCHASED FOR RESALE	$ (1,436.00)
SALARIES AND WAGES	EMPLOYEE WAGES	$ (2,187.63)
RENT AND UTILITIES	RENT PAID OR UTILITIES PAID	$ (980.00)
OTHER EXPENSES	ANY OTHER EXPENSES	$ (157.60)
RECEIVABLES	MONEY PAID BY CUSTOMERS	$ 50,588.75
INTEREST AND DIVIDENDS	BANK INTEREST	$ -
OTHER INCOME	ANY OTHER INCOME	$ 281.75

Now we simply right click on one of the highlighted cells, select Delete, then select Delete Table Rows.

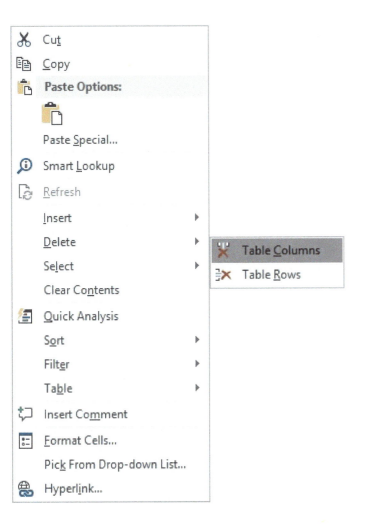

	A	B	C
1	Account ▼	Description ▼	Total Amount ▼
2	COST OF GOODS	ITEMS PURCHASED FOR RESALE	$ (1,436.00)
3			
4			
5			
6			
7			
8			

Now if you look back at our Mr. Smith's worksheet on page 47 (alternately you can view the *Ledger* worksheet and see the two Accounts), we only have two accounts, Operating and Payroll. In cell A2 on the *Accounts* worksheet, type OPERATING and press **Tab** on your keyboard. Notice the formula in cell C2 changes to $-. That's because the formula is still written for the Category information. In cell B2 type OPERATING INCOME/EXPENSES.

Excel Genius - Level 1 - Ledger Path

Renaming Named Ranges

Excel Genius - Level 1 - Ledger Path

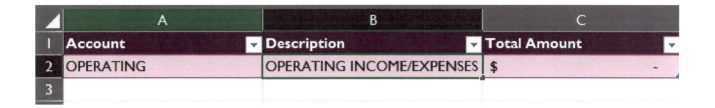

In order to change this to reflect accounts we have to do a couple things. Remember how Mr. Smith wanted the Account field in the *Ledger* worksheet to be validated? We'll start there.

Select Cell A2 again. Click on the Formula tab on the Ribbon.

Click on Name Manager.

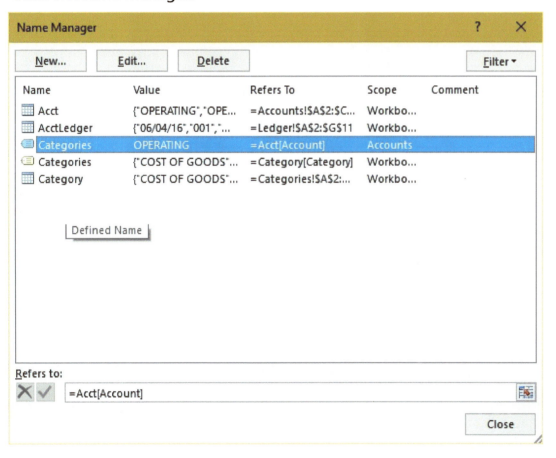

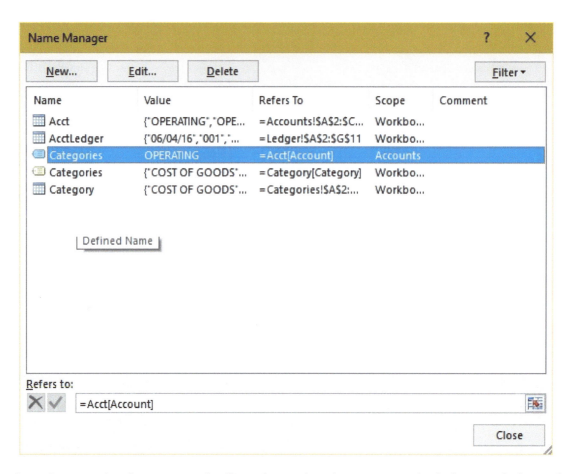

Notice that Categories is automatically selected. When we copied the worksheet for *Categories*, it also copied the named range we setup for Categories. Notice that the value is OPERATING and the Refers To column reads =Acct[Account] and it is in the Accounts worksheet. This actually makes it very easy to change the name. Simply click the Edit button at the top of the dialog.

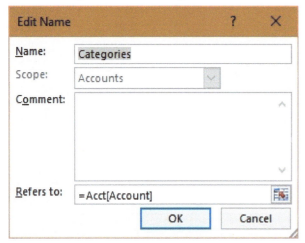

Change the Name to Account and press OK.

Excel Genius - Level 1 - Ledger Path

Rewriting Formulas

Excel Genius - Level 1 - Ledger Path

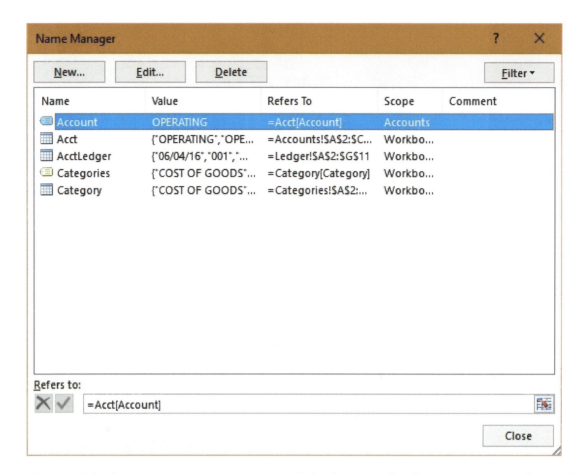

Now we are done with the name manager. Just click close at the bottom right of the dialog box.

The only thing left to do is change the Total Amount formula to reflect Accounts. Let's take a look at the formula that is currently entered in that field.

=SUMIF(AcctLedger[Category],Account,AcctLedger[Amount])

Notice that our range is still point to the Category column of our AcctLedger table. Also take note that our Criteria has already changed to *Account*. This is because we changed the name of the named range Excel copied to this worksheet. Thank you Microsoft. The Sum_Range is actually still pointing to the correct field since we want to look at the total amount by account. The only piece of the formula we need to change at this point is the Range.

Click on Cell C2. Press **F2** on your keyboard. This takes you into Edit Mode for that cell. Use your mouse to click right before the C in Category. Press your **DELETE** key on your keyboard to remove the word Category, ensuring you leave the "[ ]". Do not press enter. Your formula should now read as follows:

SUMIF(AcctLedger[],Account,AcctLedger[Amount])

In between the Brackets "[ ]", type Account. Now press enter and your formula is complete.

	A	B	C
1	Account	Description	Total Amount
2	OPERATING	OPERATING INCOME/EXPENSES	$ 48,296.90
3			

Your formula is now looking at the *Ledger* worksheet in the table *AcctLedger*. It is looking for the word OPERATING in that table in the Accounts column. It is providing a sum for any rows of data that contain OPERATING in the Accounts column from the Amount Column. Sounds pretty exhausting, and it would be if you had to do it by hand. Thank Microsoft for doing this all in milliseconds for us. Select Cell C2 and press **TAB** on your keyboard to insert a new row**.** Type PAYROLL in cell A3. Notice the formula in Cell C3 found that there was is a total of $(2187.63) in that table. The () around 2187.63 is the Accounting format for a negative number. We will fix that in a moment. In Cell B3 type PAYROLL EXPENSES and press **TAB** on your keyboard.

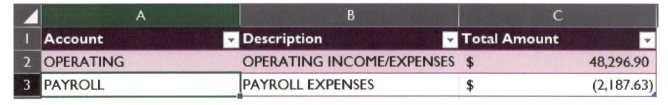

	A	B	C
1	Account	Description	Total Amount
2	OPERATING	OPERATING INCOME/EXPENSES	$ 48,296.90
3	PAYROLL	PAYROLL EXPENSES	$ (2,187.63)

Now, lets setup our data validation on the *Ledger* worksheet. Select Cells D2 through D11.

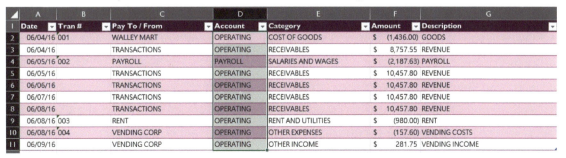

	A	B	C	D	E	F	G
1	Date	Tran #	Pay To / From	Account	Category	Amount	Description
2	06/04/16	001	WALLEY MART	OPERATING	COST OF GOODS	$ (1,436.00)	GOODS
3	06/04/16		TRANSACTIONS	OPERATING	RECEIVABLES	$ 8,757.55	REVENUE
4	06/05/16	002	PAYROLL	PAYROLL	SALARIES AND WAGES	$ (2,187.63)	PAYROLL
5	06/05/16		TRANSACTIONS	OPERATING	RECEIVABLES	$ 10,457.80	REVENUE
6	06/06/16		TRANSACTIONS	OPERATING	RECEIVABLES	$ 10,457.80	REVENUE
7	06/07/16		TRANSACTIONS	OPERATING	RECEIVABLES	$ 10,457.80	REVENUE
8	06/08/16		TRANSACTIONS	OPERATING	RECEIVABLES	$ 10,457.80	REVENUE
9	06/08/16	003	RENT	OPERATING	RENT AND UTILITIES	$ (980.00)	RENT
10	06/08/16	004	VENDING CORP	OPERATING	OTHER EXPENSES	$ (157.60)	VENDING COSTS
11	06/09/16		VENDING CORP	OPERATING	OTHER INCOME	$ 281.75	VENDING INCOME

Excel Genius - Level 1 - Ledger Path

Data Validation on Existing Data

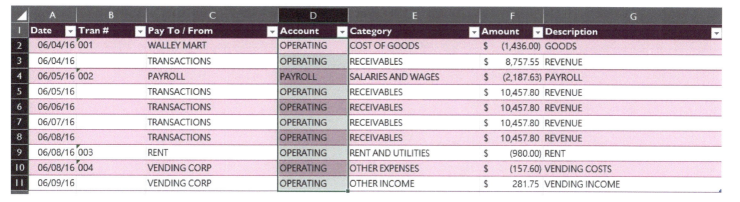

Date	Tran #	Pay To / From	Account	Category	Amount	Description
06/04/16	001	WALLEY MART	OPERATING	COST OF GOODS	$ (1,436.00)	GOODS
06/04/16		TRANSACTIONS	OPERATING	RECEIVABLES	$ 8,757.55	REVENUE
06/05/16	002	PAYROLL	PAYROLL	SALARIES AND WAGES	$ (2,187.63)	PAYROLL
06/05/16		TRANSACTIONS	OPERATING	RECEIVABLES	$ 10,457.80	REVENUE
06/06/16		TRANSACTIONS	OPERATING	RECEIVABLES	$ 10,457.80	REVENUE
06/07/16		TRANSACTIONS	OPERATING	RECEIVABLES	$ 10,457.80	REVENUE
06/08/16		TRANSACTIONS	OPERATING	RECEIVABLES	$ 10,457.80	REVENUE
06/08/16	003	RENT	OPERATING	RENT AND UTILITIES	$ (980.00)	RENT
06/08/16	004	VENDING CORP	OPERATING	OTHER EXPENSES	$ (157.60)	VENDING COSTS
06/09/16		VENDING CORP	OPERATING	OTHER INCOME	$ 281.75	VENDING INCOME

Click on the Data tab on the Ribbon.

Click on the Data Validation Icon.

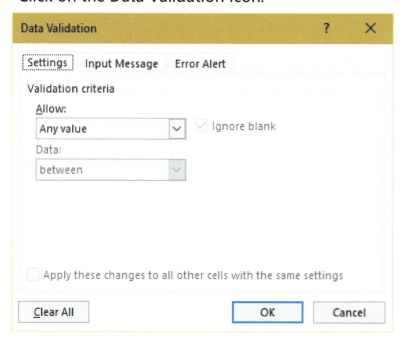

Under allow, select list

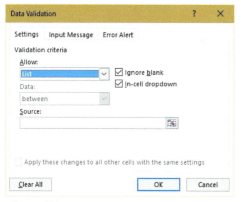

Excel Genius - Level 1 - Ledger Path

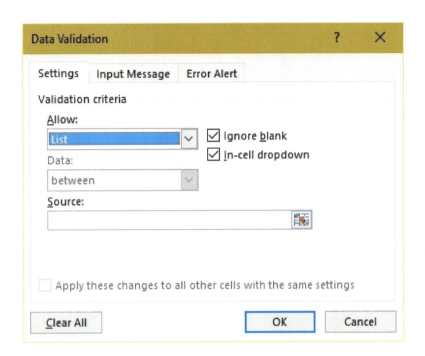

Now in source type *=Account* and press OK. You should now have drop down arrows beside the data in the accounts column when the cell is selected.

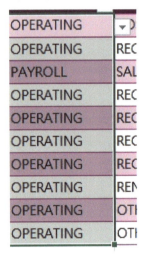

Congratulations! You have finished your workbook for Mr. Smith. Be sure to save your changes. If you email me at randy@excelgenius.co I will review your work and send you a certificate of completion, suitable for framing.

Be sure to join us for Excel Genius Training Level 2. We will explore more Formulas and Functions. We will explore custom data validation, creating charts and graphs, and we will learn to record macros to make our work easier. Remember, this entire course will utilize the workbook you just created, so don't delete it.

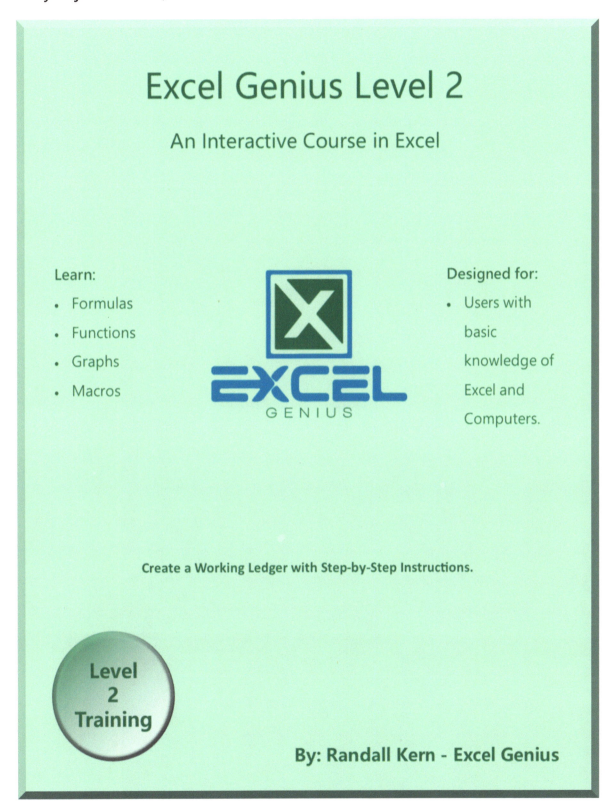

www.ingramcontent.com/pod-product-compliance
Lightning Source LLC
Chambersburg PA
CBHW041421050326
40689CB00002B/605